ArtNotes

to accompany

Art: A Brief History

SECOND EDITION

Marilyn Stokstad

PEARSON

Prentice
Hall

Upper Saddle River, New Jersey 07458

© 2004 by PEARSON EDUCATION, INC.
Upper Saddle River, New Jersey 07458

ISBN 0-13-184230-7

Printed in the United States of America

Museum credits for fine art photos can be found with the images in the text. Images in the supplement were supplied by SuperStock, Inc. Please note that where we have included artwork in ArtNotes, we have made every effort to secure the same photograph of the art that is found in your text. There are some instances, however, where we had to substitute a slightly different photograph of an object. Please consult your textbook if you are studying the objects for identification purposes.

Contents

Introduction

Notes

1 The Great Sphinx, Giza, Egypt. Dynasty 4, c. 2613–2494 BCE. *(page 13)*

2 Adriaen van der Spelt and Frans van Mieris. *Flower Piece with Curtain. (page 14)*

3 Edward Weston. *Succulent.* 1930. *(page 15)*

4 Georgia O'Keeffe. *Red Canna.* 1924. *(page 15)*

5 David Smith. *Cubi XIX.* 1964. *(page 16)*

6 Corinthian capital from the *tholos* at Epidaurus.
c. 350 BCE. *(page 17)*

7 *Medici Venus.* Roman copy of a 1st-century BCE.
(page 17)

8 Kitagawa Utamaro. *Woman at the Height of
Her Beauty.* Mid-1790s. *(page 18)*

9 *Punitavati (Karaikkalammaiyar),* Shiva saint, from Karaikka, India. 15th century. *(page 18)*

10 Cathedral of Saint James, Santiago de Compostela, Spain 1078–1122. *(page 19)*

11 Chalice of Abbot Suger, from Abbey Church of Saint-Denis France. Composite of elements from Ptolemaic Egypt (2nd–1st century BCE) and 12th-century France. 1137–40. *(page 19)*

12 James Hampton. *Throne of the Third Heaven of the Nations' Millennium General Assembly.* c. 1950–64. *(page 20)*

13 Olówè of Isè. Divination bowl. c. 1925. *(page 20)*

14 Veronese. *The Triumph of Venice,* oil on canvas in the Council Chamber, Palazzo Ducale Venice, Italy c. 1585. *(page 21)*

15 Il Guercino. *Saint Luke Displaying a Painting of the Virgin.* 1652–53. *(page 22)*

16 Dale Chihuly. *Violet Persian Set with Red Lip Wraps.* 1990. *(page 22)*

17 Jan Steen. *The Drawing Lesson.* 1665. *(page 22)*

18 Rembrandt van Rijn. *The Last Supper,* after Leonardo da Vinci's fresco. Mid-1630s. *(page 23)*

19 Leonardo da Vinci. *The Last Supper,* wall painting in the refectory, Monastery of Santa Maria delle Grazie, Milan, Italy. 1495–98. *(page 24)*

20 *Christine Presenting Her Book to the Queen of France.* 1410–15. *(page 25)*

21 James McNeill Whistler. *Harmony in Blue and Gold.*
The Peacock Room, northeast corner, from a house owned
by Frederick Leyland, London. 1876–77. *(page 25)*

22 Frank Lloyd Wright. Solomon R. Guggenheim
Museum, New York City. 1956–59. *(page 26)*

23 Lawrence Alma-Tadema. *Pheidias and the
Frieze of the Parthenon, Athens.* 1868. *(page 26)*

24 Hagesandros Polydoros, and Athanadoros of Rhodes. *Laocoön and His Sons,* as restored today Perhaps 2nd or 1st century BCE. *(page 27)*

25 Hagesandros, Polydoros, and Athanadoros of Rhodes. *Laocoön and His Sons,* an incorrect earlier restoration Perhaps 2nd or 1st century BCE, but probably a Roman copy of the 1st century CE. *(page 28)*

26 Honoré Daumier. *Rue Transonain, Le 15 Avril 1834. (page 29)*

27 Roger Shimomura. *Diary (Minidoka Series #3).*
1978. *(page 29)*

_____

_____

_____

_____

_____

_____

_____

_____

_____

_____

_____

Chapter 1
Art Before the Written Word

Notes

Wall painting with four horses. Chauvet cave,
Vallon-Pont-d'Arc, Ardèche gorge, France.
c. 28,000 BCE. *(page 31)*

_____

_____

_____

_____

_____

_____

_____

_____

_____

1-1 *Lion-Human,* from Hohlenstein-Stadel,
Germany. c. 30,000–26,000 BCE. *(page 32)*

_____

_____

_____

_____

_____

_____

_____

_____

1-2 *Woman from Brassempouy,* Grotte du Pape, Brassempouy Landes, France. c. 22,000 BCE. *(page 33)*

1-3 *Woman from Willendorf,* Austria. c. 22,000–21,000 BCE. *(page 33)*

1-4 Reconstruction drawing of mammoth-bone house from Ukraine c. 16,000–10,000 BCE. *(page 34)*

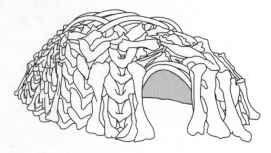

1-5 *Mimis and Kangaroo*, prehistoric rock art, Oenpelli, Arnhem Land, Australia. Older painting 16,000–7000 BCE. *(page 34)*

1-6 Wall painting with four horses, Chauvet cave, Vallon-Pont-d'Arc Ardèche gorge, France. c. 28,000 BCE. *(page 35)*

1-7 Hall of Bulls, Lascaux caves. c. 15,000–13,000 BCE. *(page 35)*

1-8 *Bison,* on the ceiling of a cave at Altamira, Spain. c. 12,000 BCE. *(page 36)*

_____
_____
_____
_____
_____
_____
_____
_____
_____
_____
_____
_____

1-9 Jomon vessel. c. 10,000 BCE. *(page 37)*

_____
_____
_____
_____
_____
_____
_____
_____
_____
_____
_____
_____

1-10 *People and Animals* detail of rock-shelter painting in Cogul Lérida, Spain c. 4000–2000 BCE. *(page 37)*

_____
_____
_____
_____
_____
_____
_____
_____
_____
_____

1-11 Plan, village of Skara Brae, Orkney Islands, Scotland By c. 3100 BCE. *(page 38)*

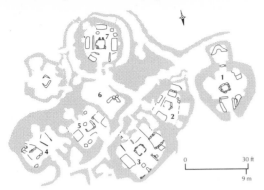

1-12 House interior Skara Brae (house 7 in fig. 1-11) *(page 38)*

1-13 Tomb interior with engraved stones, Newgrange, Ireland c. 3000–2500 BCE. *(page 39)*

1-14 Stonehenge. Salisbury Plain, Wiltshire, England. c. 2750–1500 BCE. *(page 39)*

1-15 Diagram of Stonehenge showing elements discussed in text. *(page 39)*

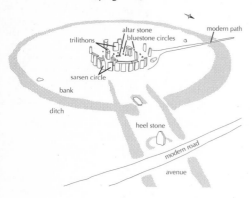

1-16 *Horse and Sun Chariot* from Trundholm Zealand Denmark. c. 1800–1600 BCE. *(page 40)*

1-17 Colossal head (no. 4), from La Venta, Mexico.
Olmec culture, c. 900–500 BCE. *(page 41)*

1-18 Ancestor figures (*moai*) Ahu Nau Nau,
Easter Island Polynesia. c. 1000–1500 CE,
restored 1978. *(page 41)*

Chapter 2
The Art of Mesopotamia and Egypt

Notes

Funerary mask of Tutankhamun (ruled 1336/35–1327 BCE), from the tomb of Tutankhamun, Valley of the Kings, Deir el-Bahri, Egypt. Photographed the day it was discovered—October 28, 1925. *(page 42)*

Funerary mask of Tutankhamun as it appears today. *(page 43)*

2-1 Reconstruction drawing of the Anu Ziggurat and White Temple, Uruk (modern Warka, Iraq). c. 3100 BCE. *(page 44)*

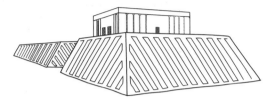

2-2 Illustration of the technique of cone mosaic. *(page 45)*

BOX Four hieroglyphs with the sounds they represent. *(page 45)*

2-3 Carved vase (two views), from Uruk (modern Warka, Iraq). c. 3500–3000 BCE. *(page 46)*

_____

_____

_____

_____

_____

_____

_____

_____

_____

_____

2-4 Nanna Ziggurat, Ur (modern Muqaiyir, Iraq). c. 2100–2050 BCE. *(page 46)*

_____

_____

_____

_____

_____

_____

_____

_____

_____

_____

2-5 Votive statues from the Square Temple, Eshnunna (modern Tell Asmar, Iraq). c. 2900–2600 BCE. *(page 47)*

_____

_____

_____

_____

_____

_____

_____

_____

_____

_____

2-6 Bull lyre, from the tomb of Queen Pu-abi, Ur (modern Muqaiyir, Iraq). c. 2680 BCE. *(page 47)*

2-7 Mythological figures, detail of the sound box of the bull lyre from the tomb of Queen Pu-abi, Ur (modern Muqaiyir, Iraq). c. 2680 BCE. *(page 48)*

2-8 Cylinder seal from Sumer and its impression. c. 2500 BCE. *(page 49)*

2-9 *Stela of Naramsin.* c. 2254–2218 BCE.
(page 49)

_____

_____

_____

_____

_____

_____

_____

_____

_____

_____

_____

_____

2-10 Votive statue of Gudea, from Lagash
(modern Telloh, Iraq). c. 2120 BCE. *(page 50)*

_____

_____

_____

_____

_____

_____

_____

_____

_____

_____

_____

2-11 *Stela of Hammurabi,* from Susa (modern
Shush, Iran). c. 1792–1750 BCE. *(page 50)*

_____

_____

_____

_____

_____

_____

_____

_____

_____

_____

_____

2-12 *Human-Headed Winged Lion (Lamassu),* from the palace of Assurnasirpal II, Nimrud. 883–859 BCE. *(page 51)*

2-13 *Assurbanipal and His Queen in the Garden* from the palace at Nineveh (modern Kuyunjik, Iraq) c. 647 BCE. *(page 51)*

2-14 *Palette of Narmer,* from Hierakonpolis Dynasty 1, c. 3150–3125 BCE. *(page 52)*

BOX *Woman Spinning,* from Susa (modern
Shush, Iran). c. 8th–7th century BCE. *(page 53)*

2-15 Stepped pyramid of Djoser, Saqqara.
(page 54)

2-16 Plan of Djoser's funerary complex Saqqara.
Dynasty 3, c. 2681–2662 BCE. *(page 54)*

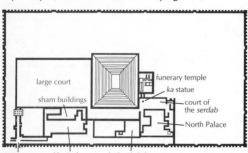

2-17 *Khafre,* from Giza. Dynasty 4, c. 2570–2544 BCE.
(page 55)

_____

_____

_____

_____

_____

_____

_____

_____

_____

_____

2-18 *Menkaure and His Wife, Queen Khamerernebty*
from Giza. Dynasty 4, c. 2515 BCE. *(page 56)*

_____

_____

_____

_____

_____

_____

_____

_____

_____

_____

_____

_____

2-19 Great Pyramids, Giza. Dynasty 4,
c. 2601–2515 BCE. *(page 57)*

_____

_____

_____

_____

_____

_____

_____

_____

_____

2-20 Plan of the funerary complex, Giza. *(page 57)*

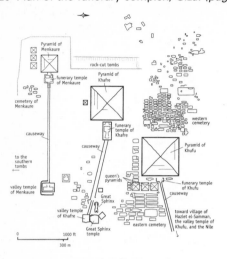

2-21 *Ti Watching a Hippopotamus Hunt.* Tomb of Ti, Saqqara Dynasty 5, c. 2510–2460 BCE. *(page 58)*

2-22 *Harvest Scene*, tempera facsimile by Nina de Garis Davies of a wall painting in the tomb of Khnumhotep, Beni Hasan. Dynasty 12, c. 1928–1895 BCE. *(page 59)*

2-23 Pectoral with the name of Senwosret II from el-Lahun. Dynasty 12, c. 1895–1878 BCE. *(page 59)*

2-24 Funerary temple of Hatshepsut, Deir el-Bahri Dynasty 18, c. 1478–1458 BCE. At the far left are the ramp and base of the funerary temple of Mentuhotep I. Dynasty 11, c. 2009–1997 BCE. *(page 60)*

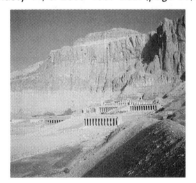

2-25 Plan of the funerary temple of Hatshepsut. Deir el-Bahri. *(page 60)*

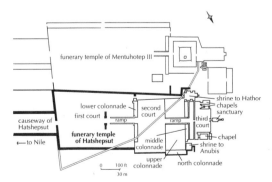

2-26 Plan of the Great Temple of Amun
Karnak. New Kingdom. *(page 60)*

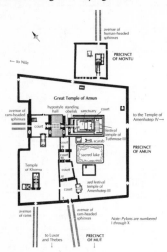

2-27 Reconstruction drawing of the hypostyle
hall Great Temple of Amun, Karnak. Dynasty
19 c. 1294–1212 BCE. *(page 61)*

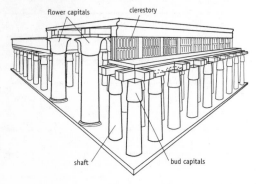

2-28 Hypostyle hall, Great Temple of Amun,
Karnak. *(page 61)*

2-29 Pylon of Ramesses II with obelisk in the foreground, Temple of Amun, Mut, and Khonsu, Luxor. Dynasty 19, c. 1279–1212 BCE. *(page 61)*

_____

_____

_____

_____

_____

_____

_____

_____

_____

_____

_____

2-30 *Queen Nefertari Making an Offering to Isis,* wall painting in the tomb of Nefertari, Valley of the Queens near Deir el-Bahri. Dynasty 19, c. 1279–1212 BCE. *(page 62)*

_____

_____

_____

_____

_____

_____

_____

_____

_____

_____

_____

_____

2-31 *Akhenaten and His Family,* from Akhetaten (modern Tell el-Amarna). Dynasty 18, 1348–1336/5 BCE. *(page 62)*

_____

_____

_____

_____

_____

_____

_____

_____

_____

_____

_____

2-32 *Queen Tiy,* from Kom Mendinet Ghurab (near el-Lahun). Dynasty 18, c. 1390–1352 BCE. *(page 63)*

2-33 *Nefertiti,* from Akhetaten (modern Tell el-Amarna). Dynasty 18, c. 1348–1336/5 BCE. *(page 63)*

2-34 Inner coffin of Tutankhamun's sarcophagus, from the tomb of Tutankhamun, Valley of the Kings. Dynasty 18, 1336/5–1327 BCE. *(page 64)*

2-35 *Judgment before Osiris,* illustration from
a Book of the Dead. Dynasty 19, c. 1285 BCE.
(page 64)

_____

_____

_____

_____

_____

_____

_____

_____

_____

_____

_____

2-36 Sphinx of Taharqo, from Temple T, Kawa,
Nubia. Dynasty 25, c. 690–664 BCE. *(page 65)*

_____

_____

_____

_____

_____

_____

_____

_____

_____

_____

_____

Chapter 3
Early Asian Art

Soldiers, from the mausoleum of the first
emperor of Qun, Lintong Shaanxi. Qin dynasty,
c. 210 BCE. *(page 66)*

_____

_____

_____

_____

_____

_____

_____

_____

_____

3-1 Seal impressions, from the Indus Valley
civilization: **a., d.** horned animal; **b.** buffalo;
c. sacrificial rite to a goddess (?); **e.** yogi;
f. three-headed animal. c. 2500–1500 BCE. *(page 68)*

_____

_____

_____

_____

_____

_____

_____

_____

_____

_____

3-2 Lion capital, from an Ashokan pillar at
Sarnath, Uttar Pradesh India. Maurya period,
c. 250 BCE. *(page 70)*

_____

_____

_____

_____

_____

_____

_____

_____

_____

_____

_____

3-3 Great Stupa Sanchi, Madhya Pradesh, India.
Founded 3rd century BCE. Enlarged c. 150–50 BCE.
(page 70)

_____

_____

_____

_____

_____

_____

_____

_____

_____

_____

3-4 North torana of the Great Stupa at Sanchi. Early
Andhra period mid-1st century BCE. *(page 71)*

_____

_____

_____

_____

_____

_____

_____

_____

_____

3-5 *Standing Buddha,* from Gandhara (Pakistan).
Kushan period, c. 2nd–3rd century CE. *(page 72)*

_____

_____

_____

_____

_____

_____

_____

_____

_____

_____

3-6 *Buddha and Attendants,* from Katra Keshavdev,
Mathura Madhya Pradesh, India. Kushan period,
c. late 1st–early 2nd century CE. *(page 72)*

_____

_____

_____

_____

_____

_____

_____

_____

_____

3-7 *Bodhisattva,* detail of a wall painting in
Cave I, Ajanta, Maharashtra, India. Gupta
period, c. 475 CE. *(page 74)*

_____

_____

_____

_____

_____

_____

_____

_____

_____

_____

3-8 Cave-Temple of Shiva at Elephanta, Maharashtra, India. Mid-6th century CE. *(page 75)*

3-9 *Eternal Shiva,* rock-cut relief in the Cave-Temple of Shiva at Elephant. Mid-6th century CE. *(page 75)*

3-10 *Fang ding,* from Tomb 1004, Houjiazhuang, Anyang, Henan Shang dynasty, Anyang period. c. 12th century BCE. *(page 77)*

3-11 Soldiers, from the mausoleum of the first emperor of Qin, Lintong Shaanxi. Qin dynasty, c. 210 BCE. *(page 77)*

3-12 Incense burner, from the tomb of Prince Liu Sheng Mancheng, Hebei. Han dynasty, 113 BCE. *(page 78)*

3-13 Detail from a rubbing of a relief in the Wu family shrine (Wuliangci), Jiaxiang, Shandong. Han dynasty, 151 CE. *(page 79)*

3-14 Seated Buddha Cave 20, Yungang Datong, Shanxi. Northern Wei dynasty, c. 460 CE. *(page 79)*

3-15 *Camel Carrying a Group of Musicians* from a tomb near Xi'an, Shanxi. Tang dynasty c. mid-8th century CE. *(page 80)*

BOX Wang Xizhi. Portion of a letter from the *Feng Ju* album. Six Dynasties period, mid-4th century CE. *(page 81)*

3-16 Nanchan Temple, Wutaishan, Shanxi.
Tang dynasty, 782 CE. *(page 81)*

3-17 Great Wild Goose Pagoda at Ci'en Temple,
Xi'an, Shanxi Tang dynasty, first erected 645 CE;
rebuilt mid-8th century CE. *(page 82)*

3-18 *Haniwa* from Kyoto Kofun period 6th
century CE. *(page 83)*

3-19 Inner Shrine, Ise, Mie Prefecture. Early
1st century CE; rebuilt 1993. *(page 84)*

3-20 Main compound Horyu-ji, Nara Prefecture.
Asuka period 7th century CE. *(page 85)*

3-21 *Hungry Tigress Jataka,* panel of the
Tamamushi Shrine, Horyu-ji. Asuka period
7th century CE. *(page 85)*

Chapter 4
Art of the Aegean World

Notes

Kallikrates and Iktinos. Parthenon. Acropolis, Athens. 447–438 BCE. *(page 86)*

_____

_____

_____

_____

_____

_____

_____

_____

_____

_____

_____

4-1 *Seated Harp Player,* from Keros, Cyclades. c. 2800–2700 BCE. *(page 90)*

_____

_____

_____

_____

_____

_____

_____

_____

_____

_____

_____

_____

_____

4-2 Reconstruction of the palace complex, Knossos, Crete. Site occupied 2000–1375 BCE; complex begun in Old Palace period (c. 1900–1700 BCE); complex rebuilt after earthquakes and fires during Second Palace period (c. 1700–1450 BCE); final destruction c. 1375 BCE. *(page 92)*

4-3 *Young Girl Gathering Crocus Flowers*, detail of wall painting, Room 3 of House Xeste 3 Akrotiri, Thera. Second Palace period, C. 1700–1450 BCE. *(page 93)*

4-4 *Bull Jumping,* wall painting with areas of
modern reconstruction, from the palace complex,
Knossos, Crete. c. 1550–1450 BCE. *(page 94)*

4-5 *Octopus Flask,* from Palaikastro, Crete.
c. 1500–1450 BCE. *(page 94)*

4-6 Pendant in the form of two bees or
wasps from Chryssolakkos near Mallia, Crete
c. 1700–1550 BCE. *(page 95)*

4-7 Dagger blade from Shaft Grave IV Grave Circle A, Mycenae Greece. c. 1600–1550 BCE. *(page 95)*

4-8 Cutaway drawing of the beehive tomb called the Treasury of Atreus, Mycenae, Greece. c. 1300–1200 BCE. *(page 96)*

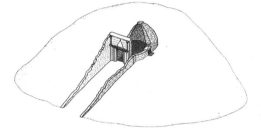

4-9 Corbeled vault, interior of the so-called Treasury of Atreus. *(page 96)*

4-10 Mycenae, Greece. c. 1600–1200 BCE.
(page 97)

_____

_____

_____

_____

_____

_____

_____

_____

_____

_____

_____

_____

4-11 Lion Gate, Mycenae. c. 1250 BCE. *(page 97)*

_____

_____

_____

_____

_____

_____

_____

_____

_____

_____

_____

_____

_____

4-12 Krater, attributed to the Hirschfeld
Workshop, Athens. c. 750–700 BCE. *(page 98)*

_____

_____

_____

_____

_____

_____

_____

_____

_____

_____

4-13 *Man and Centaur,* perhaps from Olympia.
c. 750 BCE. *(page 98)*

4-14 Corner view of the Temple of Hera I
Paestum, Italy. c. 550 BCE. *(page 99)*

4-15 Plan of the Temple of Hera I, Paestum.
(page 99)

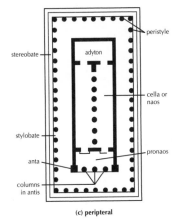

(c) peripteral

Temple of Hera I,
Paestum, Italy, c. 550 BCE
(figs. 5-9, 5-10)

4-16 Reconstruction of the west pediment of the
Temple of Artemis, Korkyra (Corfu), after
G. Rodenwaldt. c. 600–580 BCE. *(page 101)*

4-17 *Medusa*, fragments of sculpture from
the west pediment of the Temple of Artemis,
Korkyra. c. 580 BCE. *(page 101)*

4-18 *Kouros.* c. 600 BCE. *(page 102)*

4-19 *Peplos Kore* from the Acropolis, Athens. c. 530 BCE. *(page 102)*

4-20 Exekias. *The Suicide of Ajax* black-figure decoration on an amphora. c. 540 BCE. *(page 103)*

4-21 "A.D." Painter. *Women at a Fountain House,* black-figure decoration on a hydria. 520–510 BCE. *(page 104)*

4-22 Foundry Painter. *A Bronze Foundry,* red-figure decoration on a kylix from Vulci, Italy. 490–480 BCE. *(page 105)*

_____

_____

_____

_____

_____

_____

_____

_____

_____

_____

_____

4-23 Pan Painter. *Artemis Slaying Actaeon,* red-figure decoration on a bell krater. c. 470 BCE. *(page 105)*

_____

_____

_____

_____

_____

_____

_____

_____

_____

_____

_____

4-24 *Kritios Boy.* c. 480 BCE. *(page 106)*

_____

_____

_____

_____

_____

_____

_____

_____

_____

4-25 *Charioteer,* from the Sanctuary of Apollo, Delphi. c. 470 BCE. *(page 107)*

4-26 *Young Warrior* found in the sea off Riace, Italy. c. 460–450 BCE. *(page 108)*

4-27 Model of the Acropolis, Athens. c. 400 BCE. *(page 109)*

4-28 Kallikrates and Iktinos. Parthenon, Acropolis, Athens. 447–438 BCE. *(page 109)*

4-29 Photographic mock-up of the east pediment of the Parthenon (using photographs of the extant marble sculpture of c. 438–432 BCE). The blank vertical spaces represent the missing sculptures. *(page 110)*

4-30 *Lapith Fighting a Centaur* metope relief from the Doric frieze on the south side of the Parthenon c. 440 BCE. *(page 110)*

4-31 *Marshals and Young Women,* detail of the
Procession, from the Ionic frieze on the east side of
the Parthenon. c. 438–432 BCE. *(page 111)*

4-32 Mnesikles. Erechtheion, Acropolis, Athens.
c. 430–405 BCE. *(page 112)*

4-33 Porch of the Maidens (Caryatid Porch) Erechtheion
Acropolis, Athens. 421–405 BCE. *(page 112)*

4-34 *Nike (Victory) Adjusting Her Sandal,*
fragment of relief decoration from the parapet
(now destroyed). Temple of Athena Nike,
Acropolis, Athens. 410–407 BCE. *(page 113)*

4-35 Polykleitos. *Spear Bearer (Doryphoros)*
Roman copy after the original bronze of
c. 450–440 BCE. *(page 114)*

4-36 Followers of Praxiteles. *Hermes and the Infant
Dionysos,* probably a Roman copy after an original of
c. 300–250 BCE. *(page 115)*

BOX *A Vase Painter and Assistants Crowned by Athena and Victories* composite photograph of the red-figure decoration on a hydria from Athens. c. 450 BCE. *(page 116)*

4-37 *Alexander the Great,* head from a Hellenistic copy (c. 200 BCE) of a statue possibly after a 4th-century BCE original by Lysippos. *(page 117)*

Chapter 5
The Spread of Greek Art and Culture

Notes

Nike (Victory) of Samothrace from the Sanctuary of the Great Gods, Samothrace. c. 190 BCE (?). *(page 118)*

_____

_____

_____

_____

_____

_____

_____

_____

_____

_____

5-1 *She-Wolf.* c. 500 BCE. *(page 120)*

_____

_____

_____

_____

_____

_____

_____

_____

_____

_____

5-2 *Apollo,* from Veii. c. 500 BCE. *(page 121)*

5-3 Reconstruction of an Etruscan temple
based partly on descriptions by Vitruvius
University of Rome, Istituto de Etruscologia e
Antichità Italiche. *(page 122)*

5-4 Burial chamber, Tomb of the Reliefs, Cerveteri.
3rd century BCE. *(page 122)*

5-5 *Musicians and Dancers,* detail of a wall
painting, Tomb of the Lionesses, Tarquinia.
c. 480–470 BCE. *(page 123)*

5-6 Sarcophagus, from Cerveteri. c. 520 BCE.
(page 124)

5-7 *Scythian Stag,* shield plaque. Late 7th–early
6th century BCE. *(page 124)*

5-8 Reconstruction drawing of Babylon in the
6th century BCE. *(page 125)*

5-9 Ishtar Gate and throne room wall, from
Babylon (Iraq). c. 575 BCE. *(page 126)*

5-10 Daric, a coin first minted under Darius I
of Persia 4th century BCE. *(page 127)*

5-11 Apadana (Audience Hall) of Darius I and
Xerxes I, ceremonial complex, Persepolis, Iran.
518–c. 460 BCE *(page 128)*

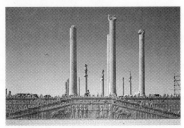

_____

_____

_____

_____

_____

_____

_____

_____

_____

_____

_____

5-12 *Darius and Xerxes Receiving Tribute,* detail of a relief
from the stairway leading to the Apadana, ceremonial
complex Persepolis, Iran. 491–486 BCE. *(page 129)*

_____

_____

_____

_____

_____

_____

_____

_____

_____

_____

_____

_____

BOX Plan of the theater at Epidauros *(page 129)*

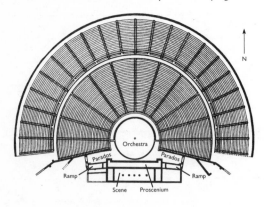

_____

_____

_____

_____

_____

_____

_____

_____

_____

_____

5-13 *Aphrodite of Melos* (also called *Venus de Milo*). c. 150 BCE. *(page 130)*

_____

_____

_____

_____

_____

_____

_____

_____

_____

_____

_____

5-14 *Market Woman.* 1st century BCE. *(page 130)*

_____

_____

_____

_____

_____

_____

_____

_____

_____

_____

_____

_____

_____

_____

_____

5-15 *Nike (Victory) of Samothrace,* from the Sanctuary of the Great Gods, Samothrace. c. 190 BCE (?). *(page 131)*

_____

_____

_____

_____

_____

_____

_____

_____

_____

5-16 Epigonos (?). *Dying Gallic Trumpeter,* Roman copy after the original bronze of c. 220 BCE. *(page 132)*

_____

_____

_____

_____

_____

_____

_____

_____

_____

_____

5-17 Reconstructed west front of the altar from Pergamon, Turkey. c. 166–159 BCE. *(page 133)*

_____

_____

_____

_____

_____

_____

_____

_____

_____

_____

_____

5-18 *Athena Attacking the Giants,* detail of the frieze from the east front of the altar from Pergamon. *(page 134)*

_____

_____

_____

_____

_____

_____

_____

_____

_____

_____

5-19 *Alexander the Great Confronts Darius III at the Battle of Issos,* Roman mosaic copy after a Greek painting of c. 310 BCE, perhaps by Philoxenos or Helen of Egypt. *(page 135)*

Chapter 6
Art of the Roman Republic and Empire

Notes

Heraklitos. *The Unswept Floor,* mosaic variant of a 2nd-century BCE painting by Sosos of Pergamon. 2nd century CE. *(page 136)*

_____

_____

_____

_____

_____

_____

_____

_____

_____

_____

6-1 *Aulus Metellus* found near Perugia. Late 2nd or early 1st century BCE. *(page 138)*

_____

_____

_____

_____

_____

_____

_____

_____

_____

6-2 Temple perhaps dedicated to Portunus, Forum Boarium (cattle market), Rome. Late 2nd century BCE. *(page 139)*

6-3 Plan of the temple perhaps dedicated to Portunus. *(page 139)*

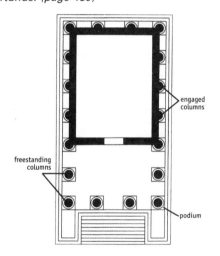

engaged columns

freestanding columns

podium

6-4 Reconstruction drawing and plan of the House of Pansa Pompeii. 2nd century BCE. *(page 140)*

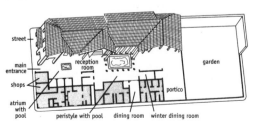

street

main entrance

shops

atrium with pool

reception room

peristyle with pool   dining room   winter dining room

garden

portico

6-5 Atrium, House of the Silver Wedding,
Pompeii. Early 1st century CE. *(page 140)*

_____

_____

_____

_____

_____

_____

_____

_____

_____

6-6 Pont du Gard, Nîmes, France. Late 1st
century BCE. *(page 141)*

_____

_____

_____

_____

_____

_____

_____

_____

_____

6-7 *Augustus of Primaporta.* Early 1st century CE
(perhaps a copy of a bronze statue of c. 20 BCE).
(page 142)

_____

_____

_____

_____

_____

_____

_____

_____

_____

_____

6-8 Ara Pacis. 13–9 BCE. *(page 143)*

6-9 *Imperial Procession,* detail of a relief on the Ara Pacis. *(page 144)*

6-10 *Gemma Augustea.* Early 1st century CE. *(page 145)*

6-11 Colosseum, Rome. 72–80 CE. *(page 146)*

_____

_____

_____

_____

_____

_____

_____

_____

_____

_____

_____

6-12 Colosseum. *(page 146)*

_____

_____

_____

_____

_____

_____

_____

_____

_____

_____

_____

6-13 Arch of Titus, Rome. c. 81 CE. *(page 147)*

_____

_____

_____

_____

_____

_____

_____

_____

_____

_____

_____

6-14 *Spoils from the Temple of Solomon, Jerusalem,* relief in the passageway of the Arch of Titus. *(page 148)*

6-15 *Young Flavian Woman.* c. 90 CE. *(page 148)*

6-16 *Young Woman Writing,* detail of a wall painting from Pompeii. Late 1st century CE. *(page 149)*

6-17 Detail of a wall painting in the House of M. Lucretius Fronto, Pompeii. Mid-1st century CE *(page 150)*

_____

_____

_____

_____

_____

_____

_____

_____

_____

6-18 *Garden Scene* detail of a wall painting from the Villa of Livia at Primaporta, near Rome. Late 1st century BCE *(page 151)*

_____

_____

_____

_____

_____

_____

_____

_____

_____

_____

6-19 *Initiation Rites of the Cult of Bacchus (?)* detail of a wall painting in the Villa of the Mysteries, Pompeii. c. 50 BCE *(page 151)*

_____

_____

_____

_____

_____

_____

_____

_____

_____

6-20 Heraklitos. *The Unswept Floor* mosaic variant of a 2nd-century BCE painting by Sosos of Pergamon. 2nd century CE. *(page 152)*

6-21 Model of the Forum Romanum and Imperial Forums, Rome. c. 46 BCE–325 CE. *(page 153)*

6-22 Pantheon, Rome. 125–28 CE. *(page 154)*

6-23 Reconstruction drawing of the Pantheon.
(page 155)

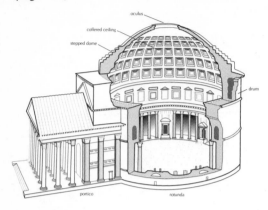

6-24 Dome of the Pantheon with light from
oculus on its coffered ceiling. *(page 155)*

6-25 *Hadrian Hunting Boar* and *Sacrificing to
Apollo.* Roundels made for a monument to Hadrian
and reused on the Arch of Constantine Sculpture.
c. 130–38 CE. *(page 156)*

6-26 *Marcus Aurelius.* 161–80 CE. *(page 156)*

6-27 *Commodus as Hercules,* from Esquiline Hill, Rome. 191–92 CE. *(page 157)*

6-28 Hadrian's Wall, seen near Housesteads, England. 2nd century CE. *(page 158)*

6-29 Openwork box lid from Cornalaragh, County Monaghan, Ireland. La Tène period c. 1st century BCE. *(page 159)*

6-30 Plan and isometric reconstruction of the Basilica of Maxentius and Constantine, Rome (constructed 306–13 CE). *(page 159)*

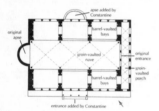

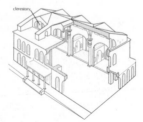

6-31 *Constantine the Great,* from the Basilica of Maxentius and Constantine, Rome. 325–26 CE. *(page 160)*

6-32 Basilica of Maxentius and Constantine.
(page 160)

6-33 Arch of Constantine, Rome. 312–15 CE
(dedicated July 25, 315 CE). *(page 161)*

Chapter 7
Jewish, Early Christian, and Byzantine Art

Notes

Cubiculum of Leonis, Catacomb of Commodilla, near Rome. Late 4th century. *(page 164)*

7-1 *Menorahs and Ark of the Covenant,* wall painting in a Jewish catacomb, Villa Torlonia, Rome. 3rd century. *(page 166)*

7-2 Wall with Torah niche, from a house-synagogue,
Dura-Europos Syria. 244–45. *(page 166)*

7-3 Synagogue floor, Maon c. 530. *(page 167)*

7-4 *Cubiculum of Leonis, Catacomb of Commodilla,
near Rome. Late 4th century. (page 170)*

7-5 Reconstruction drawing of Old Saint Peter's, Rome c. 320–27; atrium added in later 4th century. For plan see "Basilica-Plan and Central-Plan Churches," opposite. *(page 170)*

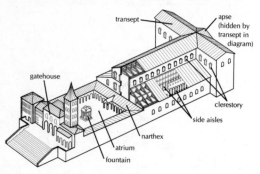

7-6 Church of Santa Sabina, Rome, 422–32. *(page 172)*

7-7 Interior Church of Santa Sabina. View from the sanctuary to the entrance. *(page 172)*

7-8 *Parting of Lot and Abraham,* mosaic in the
nave arcade, Church of Santa Maria Maggiore,
Rome, 432–40. *(page 173)*

7-9 Mausoleum of Galla Placidia, Ravenna, Italy.
c. 425–26. *(page 173)*

7-10 *Good Shepherd,* mosaic in the lunette
over the west entrance, Mausoleum of Galla
Placidia, Ravenna, Italy. c. 425–26. *(page 174)*

7-11 Anthemius of Tralles and Isidorus of Miletus. Church of Hagia Sophia, Istanbul, Turkey. 532–37. *(page 175)*

7-12 Plan and section of the Church of Hagia Sophia. *(page 175)*

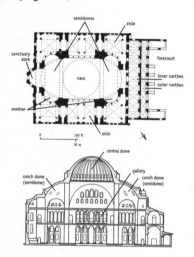

7-13 Church of Hagia Sophia *(page 176)*

7-14 Plan and cutaway drawing of the Church of San Vitale Ravenna, Italy. 526–47. *(page 177)*

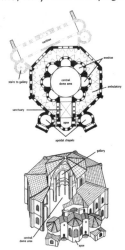

7-15 Church of San Vitale. View across the central space toward the sanctuary apse with mosaic showing Christ enthroned and flanked by Saint Vitalis and Bishop Ecclesius. *(page 177)*

7-16 *Empress Theodora and Her Attendants*, mosaic on south wall of the apse, Church of San Vitale. c. 547. *(page 178)*

7-17 *The Transfiguration of Christ with Saint Apollinaris, First Bishop of Ravenna,* mosaic in the apse Church of Sant'Apollinare in Classe, the former port of Ravenna (Classis), Italy. 533–49. *(page 179)*

7-18 Page with *The Crucifixion,* from the *Rabbula Gospels* from Beth Zagba, Syria. 586. *(page 181)*

7-19 *Virgin and Child with Saints and Angels,* icon, Monastery of Saint Catherine, Mount Sinai, Egypt. Second half of 6th century. *(page 181)*

7-20 Plan of the Cathedral of San Marco, Venice. Begun 1063. *(page 182)*

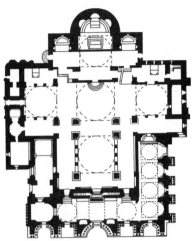

7-21 Cathedral of San Marco, Venice. Present building begun 1063. View looking toward apse. *(page 182)*

7-22 Central dome and apse, Katholikon Monastery of Hosios Loukas near Stiris, Greece. Early 11th century and later. *(page 183)*

7-23 Interior, Cathedral of Santa Sophia, Kiev,
Ukraine. 11th century and later. *(page 184)*

7-24 *Archangel Michael,* icon. 10th century.
(page 185)

7-25 *Anastasis,* painting in the apse of the funerary
chapel, Church of the Monastery of Christ in Chora.
Istanbul, Turkey. Early 14th century. *(page 186)*

7-26 Andrey Rublyov. *The Old Testament Trinity (Three Angels Visiting Abraham)*, icon. c. 1410–20. *(page 187)*

Chapter 8
Islamic Art

Shazi. Pen box, from Persia (Iran). c. 1210–11. *(page 188)*

8-1 Page from Koran (*surah* II: 286 and title *surah* III) in kufic script, from Syria or Iraq. 9th century. *(page 190)*

BOX *The Prophet Muhammad and His Companions Traveling to the Fair* from a later copy of the *Siyar-i Nabi* (*Life of the Prophet*) of al-Zarir (14th century), Istanbul, Turkey. 1594. *(page 191)*

8-2 Dome of the Rock, Jerusalem, Israel. Begun 692. *(page 192)*

8-3 Cutaway drawing of the Dome of the Rock. *(page 192)*

8-4 Dome of the Rock Jerusalem, Israel
Interior. Begun 692. *(page 193)*

_____

_____

_____

_____

_____

_____

_____

_____

_____

_____

8-5 The Great Mosque. Kairouan, Tunisia.
836–875. *(page 194)*

_____

_____

_____

_____

_____

_____

_____

_____

_____

_____

_____

_____

8-6 Prayer hall, Great Mosque, Córdoba,
Spain. Begun 785–86. *(page 195)*

_____

_____

_____

_____

_____

_____

_____

_____

_____

8-7 Dome in front of the *mihrab*, Great Mosque. 965. *(page 195)*

8-8 Emeterius and Ende, with the scribe Senior. Page with *Battle of the Bird and the Serpent. Commentary on the Apocalypse* by Beatus and *Commentary on Daniel* by Jerome, made for Abbot Dominicus, probably at the Monastery of San Salvador at Tábara, León, Spain. Completed July 6, 975. *(page 196)*

8-9 Bowl with kufic border, Samarkand, Uzbekistan. 9th–10th century. *(page 197)*

8-10 Courtyard, Masjid-i Jami (Great Mosque), Isfahan,
Persia (Iran) 11th–18th century. *(page 197)*

_____

_____

_____

_____

_____

_____

_____

_____

_____

_____

8-11 Tile mosaic *Mihrab*, from the Madrasa Imami,
Isfahan, Persia (Iran). c. 1354. (restored). *(page 198)*

_____

_____

_____

_____

_____

_____

_____

_____

_____

_____

8-12 *Qibla* wall with *mihrab* and *minbar*, main *iwan*
(vaulted chamber) in a mosque, Sultan Hasan *madrasa-*
mausoleum-mosque, Cairo Egypt. 1356–63. *(page 198)*

_____

_____

_____

_____

_____

_____

_____

_____

_____

_____

8-13 Court of the Lions, Palace of the Lions (Palacio de los Leones), Alhambra, Granada, Spain. Begun c. 1380. *(page 199)*

8-14 *Muqarnas* dome, Hall of the Abencerrajes, Palace of the Lions. *(page 200)*

8-15 Bottle, from Syria Mid-14th century. *(page 201)*

8-16 Shazi. Pen box, from Persia (Iran). 1210–11. *(page 202)*

8-17 *Bahram Gur with the Indian Princess in Her Black Pavilion.* Folio 23 from a *Haft Paykar* (*Seven Portraits*), by Nizami. 15th century. Herat Afghanistan. c. 1426. *(page 203)*

8-18 Page with *Hamza's Spies Scale the Fortress* from the *Hamza-nama*, North India. Mughal period, Mughal, reign of Akbar, c. 1567–82. *(page 204)*

8-19 Taj Mahal, Agra, India. Mughal period, Mughal, reign of Shah Jahan, c. 1632–48 *(page 205)*

8-20 Sinan. Selimiye Cami (Mosque of Selim), Edirne, Turkey. 1570–74 *(page 206)*

8-21 Illuminated *tughra* of Sultan Suleyman, from Istanbul, Turkey. c. 1555. *(page 207)*

Chapter 9
Later Asian Art

Notes

Stone and gravel garden, Ryoan-ji Kyoto.
Muromachi period, c. 1480. *(page 208)*

_____

_____

_____

_____

_____

_____

_____

_____

_____

_____

_____

9-1 Schematic drawing of the two main Indian
temple forms: northern style (left), and
southern style (right). *(page 210)*

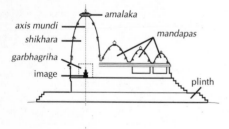

_____

_____

_____

_____

_____

_____

_____

_____

_____

_____

_____

9-2 Kandariya Mahadeva temple. Khajuraho Madhya Pradesh, India. Chandella dynasty, Early Medieval period, c. 1000 CE. *(page 210)*

9-3 Rajarajeshvara Temple to Shiva, Thanjavur, Tamil Nadu, India. Chola dynasty, Early Medieval period, 1003–1010 CE. *(page 211)*

9-4 *Nataraja: Shiva as Lord of Dance.* South India Chola dynasty, 11th century. *(page 212)*

9-5 *Hour of Cowdust,* from Punjab Hills, India. Mughal period, Rajput, Kangra school, c. 1790. *(page 213)*

9-6 Panel from a box. Tamil Nadu, India, late 17th–18th century. *(page 214)*

9-7 Seated Guanyin Bodhisattva. Liao dynasty, 11th–12th century. *(page 215)*

9-8 Fan Kuan. *Travelers among Mountains and Streams.* Northern Song dynasty, early 11th century. *(page 216)*

9-9 Xia Gui. *Detail of Twelve Views from a Thatched Hut.* Southern Song dynasty, early 13th century. *(page 216-217)*

9-10 Guan Ware vase. Southern Song dynasty, 13th century. *(page 217)*

9-11 Zhao Mengfu. *Section of Autumn Colors on the Qiao and Hua Mountains.* Yuan dynasty, 1296. *(page 218)*

9-12 Shen Zhou. *Poet on a Mountain Top*, leaf from an album of landscapes; painting mounted as part of a handscroll, Ming dynasty, c. 1500. *(page 218)*

9-13 Porcelain flask with decoration in blue underglaze Ming dynasty, c. 1425–35. *(page 219)*

9-14 The Forbidden City, now the Palace Museum Beijing. Mostly Ming dynasty. *(page 220)*

9-15 Byodo-in. Uji, Kyoto Prefecture. Heian period c. 1053. *(page 221)*

9-16 Jocho. *Amida Buddha* Byodo-in. Heian period. c. 1053. *(page 222)*

9-17 Album leaf from the *Ishiyama-gire* Heian period, early 12th century. *(page 223)*

9-18 Scene from *The Tale of Genji.* Heian period, 12th century. *(page 224)*

9-19 Attributed to Kao Ninga *Monk Sewing.* Kamakura period, early 14th century. *(page 225)*

9-20 Stone and gravel garden, Ryoan-ji, Kyoto. Muromachi period, c. 1480. *(page 226)*

9-21 Kano Eitoku *Fusuma* depicting pine and cranes (left) and plum tree (right), from the central room of the Juko-in, Daitoku-ji Kyoto. Momoyama period, c. 1563–73. *(page 227)*

9-22 Hon'ami Koetsu. Teabowl, called *Mount Fuji.* Edo period, early 17th century. *(page 227)*

9-23 Suzuki Harunobu. *Geisha as Daruma Crossing the Sea.* Edo period, mid-18th century. *(page 228)*

9-24 Katsushika Hokusai. *The Great Wave.* Edo period, c. 1831. *(page 229)*

Chapter 10
Early Medieval and Romanesque Art

Notes

Page with *Christ Washing the Feet of His Disciples, Gospels of Otto III.* c. 1000. *(page 232)*

_____

_____

_____

_____

_____

_____

_____

_____

_____

_____

_____

10-1 Gummersmark brooch, Denmark. 6th century. *(page 234)*

_____

_____

_____

_____

_____

_____

_____

_____

_____

_____

_____

10-2 Purse cover, from the Sutton Hoo burial
ship, Suffolk, England. c. 615–25. *(page 235)*

10-3 *Chi Rho Iota* page, Book of Matthew,
Book of Kells probably made at Iona, Scotland.
Late 8th or early 9th century. *(page 235)*

10-4 Reconstruction drawing of the Palace Chapel
of Charlemagne, Aachen (Aix-la-Chapelle),
Germany. Constructed 792–805. *(page 236)*

10-5 Palace Chapel of Charlemagne. *(page 236)*

10-6 Plan of the Abbey of Saint Gall (redrawn).
c. 817. *(page 237)*

10-7 Model after the Saint Gall monastery
plan (see fig. 10-6). *(page 237)*

10-8 Page with *Matthew the Evangelist*. Book of
Matthew, *Ebbo Gospels*. c. 816–40. *(page 238)*

10-9 *Crucifixion with Angels and Mourning Figures,*
outer cover, *Lindau Gospels*. c. 870–80. *(page 239)*

10-10 *Christ Enthroned with Saints and Emperor
Otto I,* one of a series of nineteen ivory plaques,
known as the *Magdeburg Ivories*. German or
North Italian. c. 962–73. *(page 240)*

10-11 Bishop Bernward Doors made for the
Abbey Church of Saint Michael. Cathedral
Museum Hildesheim Germany 1015. *(page 241)*

10-12 Nave, Church of Saint Cyriakus, Gernrode.
(page 242)

10-13 Page with *Christ Washing the Feet of His
Disciples, Gospels of Otto III.* c. 1000. *(page 242)*

10-14 Presentation page with Abbess Hitda
and Saint Walpurga, *Hitda Gospels*. Early
11th century. *(page 243)*

10-15 *Christ in Majesty,* detail of apse painting
from the Church of San Clemente, Tahull
Lérida, Spain. c. 1123. *(page 244)*

10-16 Abbey Church of Sainte-Foy Conques
Rouergue, France. Mid-11th–12th century. *(page 246)*

10-17 Reliquary statue of Saint Foy (Saint Faith), made in the Auvergne region, France, for the Abbey Church of Conques, Rouergue, France. Late 9th to first half of 10th century. *(page 247)*

10-18 Plan of Abbey Church of Sainte-Foy. *(page 246)*

10-19 Nave, Abbey Church of Saint-Savin-sur-Gartempe Poitou, France. c. 1100. *(page 248)*

10-20 West portal, Cathedral (originally abbey church) of Saint-Lazare Autun, Burgundy, France. c. 1120–35/40. *(page 249)*

10-21 *The Magi Asleep,* capital from the nave, Cathedral of Saint-Lazare. c. 1120–32. *(page 250)*

10-22 *Virgin and Child in Majesty,* from Auvergne region, France. c. 1150–1200. *(page 250)*

10-23 Page with self-portrait of the nun Guda, *Book of Homilies*. Early 12th century. *(page 251)*

10-24 John of Worcester. Page with *Dream of Henry I, Worcester Chronicle,* Worcester, England. c. 1140. *(page 252)*

10-25 *Bishop Odo Blessing the Feast,* sections 47–48 of the *Bayeux Tapestry,* Norman-Anglo-Saxon embroidery from Canterbury Kent, England, or Bayeux, Normandy, France. c. 1066–82. *(page 252)*

10-26 (Castle-monastery-cathedral complex, Durham
Northumberland, England. c. 1075–1100s, plus later
alterations and additions. *(page 253)*

10-27 Plan of Durham Castle. *(page 253)*

10-28 Nave of Durham Cathedral. Early 12th
century. Original apses replaced by a Gothic
choir 1242–c. 1280. *(page 254)*

10-29 Church of Saint-Étienne, Caen,
Normandy, France. Begun 1064; facade late
11th century; spires 13th century. *(page 255)*

Chapter 11
Gothic Art

Notes

Detail from *The Life of Charlemagne* ambulatory window, Chartres Cathedral. c. 1225. *(page 256)*

_____

_____

_____

_____

_____

_____

_____

_____

_____

_____

_____

_____

Detail from *Genesis* and *The Parable of the Good Samaritan*, south aisle window, Chartres Cathedral. c. 1210. *(page 257)*

_____

_____

_____

_____

_____

_____

_____

_____

_____

_____

_____

_____

11-1 Ambulatory choir, Abbey Church of Saint-Denis. Saint-Denis, Île-de-France, France. *(page 258)*

11-2 Plan of the sanctuary, Abbey Church of Saint-Denis. 1140–44. *(page 258)*

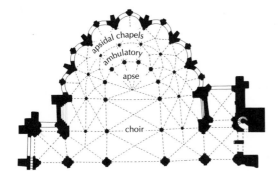

11-3 West facade, Chartres Cathedral, the Cathedral of Notre-Dame, Chartres, France. c. 1134–1220; south tower c. 1160; north spire 1507–13. *(page 259)*

11-4 Royal Portal, west facade, Chartres
Cathedral. c. 1145–55. *(page 260)*

11-5 Plan of Chartres Cathedral. c. 1194–1220.
(page 260)

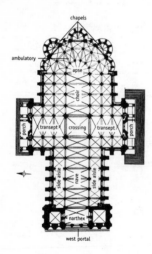

11-6 Nave, Chartres Cathedral. c. 1200–20.
(page 261)

11-7 Detail from *Genesis* and *The Parable of the Good Samaritan,* south aisle window, Chartres Cathedral. c. 1210. *(page 263)*

11-8 Detail from *The Life of Charlemagne,* ambulatory window. Chartres Cathedral. c. 1225. *(page 263)*

11-9 *Tree of Jesse,* west facade, Chartres Cathedral. c. 1150–70. *(page 264)*

11-10 Cathedral of Notre-Dame, Paris. Begun
1163. View from the southeast. *(page 265)*

11-11 West facade, Reims Cathedral. 1230s–1260;
towers mid-15th century. *(page 266)*

11-12 *Annunciation* (left pair: archangel Gabriel
c. 1255, Mary c. 1245) and *Visitation* (right pair:
c. 1230), right side, central portal, west facade,
Reims Cathedral. *(page 267)*

11-13 Interior, upper chapel, the Sainte-Chapelle, Paris. 1243–48. *(page 268)*

11-14 *Virgin and Child* from the Abbey Church of Saint-Denis. c. 1339. *(page 269)*

11-15 Page with *Louis IX and Queen Blanche of Castile,* Moralized Bible, from Paris. 1226–34. *(page 270)*

11-16 Jean Pucelle. Pages with *Betrayal and Arrest of Christ,* folio 15v. (left) and *Annunciation,* folio 16r. (right) *Petites Heures of Jeanne d'Evreux*, from Paris. c. 1325–28. *(page 271)*

11-17 Gothic castle. *(page 272)*

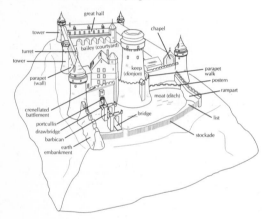

11-18 West facade, Salisbury Cathedral, Salisbury. Wiltshire, England. 1220–58; west facade 1265; spire c. 1320–30. *(page 273)*

11-19 Plan of Salisbury Cathedral. *(page 273)*

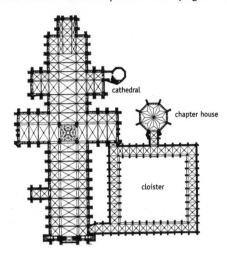

cathedral

chapter house

cloister

11-20 William Hurley Lantern Tower. Ely Cathedral, Cambridgeshire, England. 1328–47. *(page 274)*

11-21 *Life of the Virgin* (Chichester-Constable chasuble back from a set of vestments embroidered in *opus anglicanum*) from southern England. 1330–50. *(page 275)*

11-22 Interior, Altneuschul, Prague, Bohemia (Czech Republic). c. late 13th century; later additions and alterations. Engraving from Das Historisches Prag in 25 Stahlstichen, *1864.* (page 275)

11-23 Plan of Altneuschul. *(page 275)*

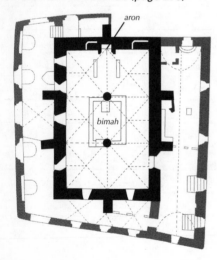

11-24 Nicola Pisano. Pulpit, Baptistry, Pisa. 1260. *(page 276)*

11-25 Andrea Pisano. *Life of John the Baptist,*
south doors, Baptistry of San Giovanni, Florence.
1330–36. *(page 277)*

11-26 Duccio de Buoninsegna. Conjectural reconstruction
of *Virgin and Child in Majesty* (*Maestà*). Original location
Siena Cathedral. 1308–11. *(page 278)*

11-27 Cimabue. *Virgin and Child Enthroned,* from the
Church of Santa Trinità, Florence. c. 1280. *(page 280)*

11-28 Giotto di Bondone. *Virgin and Child Enthroned,* from the Church of the Ognissanti, Florence. c. 1310. *(page 281)*

11-29 Giotto di Bondone. Frescoes, Arena (Scrovegni) Chapel, Padua. View toward the east wall, 1305–06. *(page 282)*

11-30 Giotto di Bondone. *Marriage at Cana, Raising of Lazarus, Resurrection and Noli Me Tangere,* and *Lamentation* (clockwise from top left), frescoes on north wall of Arena Chapel, Padua. *(page 283)*

Chapter 12
Early Renaissance Art

Notes

Paolo Uccello. *The Battle of San Romano*
(*details*). 1430s(?). *(page 286)*

_____

_____

_____

_____

_____

_____

_____

_____

_____

_____

BOX Benozzo Gozzoli. *Saint Augustine
Teaching in Rome.* 1464–65. *(page 289)*

_____

_____

_____

_____

_____

_____

_____

_____

_____

12-1 Robert Campin and assistants. *Mérode Altarpiece (Triptych of the Annunciation)* (open). c. 1425–28. *(page 289)*

12-2 Jan van Eyck. *The Annunciation.* c. 1434–36 *(page 290)*

12-3 Jan van Eyck. *Portrait of Giovanni Arnolfini (?) and His Wife, Giovanna Cenami (?).*1434. *(page 291)*

12-4 Rogier van der Weyden. *Deposition,* from an altarpiece commissioned by the Crossbowmen's Guild, Louvain, Brabant, Belgium. c. 1442. *(page 292)*

12-5 Petrus Christus. *A Goldsmith in His Shop, Possibly Saint Eligius.* 1449. *(page 293)*

12-6 Hugo van der Goes. *Portinari Altarpiece* (open). c. 1474–76. *(page 293)*

12-7 Nuño Gonçalvez. *Saint Vincent with the Portuguese Royal Family,* panel from the *Altarpiece of Saint Vincent.* c. 1471–81. *(page 294)*

_____

_____

_____

_____

_____

_____

_____

_____

_____

_____

BOX Page with Thamyris, from Giovanni Boccaccio's *De Claris Mulieribus (Concerning Famous Women).* 1402. *(page 295)*

_____

_____

_____

_____

_____

_____

_____

_____

12-8 Paul, Herman, and Jean Limbourg. Page with *February, Très Riches Heures.* 1413–16. *(page 296)*

_____

_____

_____

_____

_____

_____

_____

_____

_____

_____

12-9 *The Unicorn is Found,* from the Hunt of the Unicorn tapestry series. c. 1498–1500. *(page 297)*

12-10 Donatello. *David.* Dated as early as c. 1420 and as late as the 1460s. *(page 298)*

12-11 Donatello. Equestrian monument of Erasmo da Narni (Gattamelata), Piazza del Santo, Padua. 1443–53. *(page 298)*

12-12 Lorenzo Ghiberti. *Gates of Paradise.* (East Doors), Baptistry of San Giovanni, Florence. 1425–52. *(page 299)*

12-13 Filippo Brunelleschi. Dome of Florence Cathedral. 1417–36; lantern completed 1471. *(page 300)*

12-14 Cutaway drawing of Brunelleschi's dome, Florence Cathedral Drawing by P. Sanpaolesi. *(page 300)*

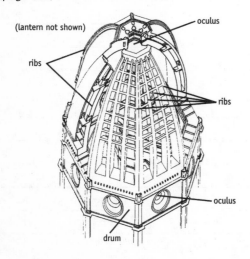

(lantern not shown)

oculus

ribs

ribs

oculus

drum

12-15 Plan of the Church of San Lorenzo including later additions and modifications. *(page 301)*

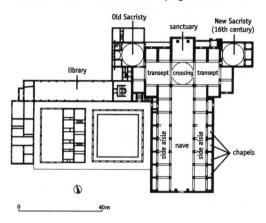

12-16 Filippo Brunelleschi Nave, Church of San Lorenzo Florence, begun c. 1421. *(page 301)*

12-17 Leon Battista Alberti. Palazzo Rucellai, Florence. 1455–70. *(page 302)*

12-18 Anonymous. *View of an Ideal City.* c. 1500. *(page 302)*

_____

_____

_____

_____

_____

_____

_____

_____

_____

_____

12-19 Masaccio.*Trinity with the Virgin, Saint John the Evangelist, and Donors* fresco in the Church of Santa Maria Novella, Florence. c. 1426–27. *(page 303)*

_____

_____

_____

_____

_____

_____

_____

_____

_____

12-20 Interior of the Brancacci Chapel, Church of Santa Maria del Carmine, Florence, with frescoes by Masaccio and Masolino (1424–27) and Filippino Lippi (c. 1482–84). *(page 304)*

_____

_____

_____

_____

_____

_____

_____

_____

_____

12-21 Masaccio. *Tribute Money,* fresco in the Brancacci Chapel, Church of Santa Maria del Carmine, Florence. c. 1427. *(page 305)*

12-22 Fra Angelico. *Annunciation,* fresco in north corridor, Monastery of San Marco, Florence, c. 1438–45. *(page 306)*

12-23 Paolo Uccello. *The Battle of San Romano.* 1430s(?). *(page 307)*

12-24 Piero della Francesca.*Battista Sforza* (left) and *Federico da Montefeltro* (right). 1472–73. *(page 308)*

12-25 Sandro Botticelli. *Birth of Venus.* c. 1484–86. *(page 309)*

12-26 Andrea Mantegna. Frescoes in the Camera Picta, Ducal Palace, Mantua. 1465–74. *(page 310)*

12-27 Giovanni Bellini. *Saint Francis in Ecstasy.* 1470s. *(page 311)*

12-28 Pietro Perugino. *Delivery of the Keys to Saint Peter* fresco in the Sistine Chapel, Vatican, Rome. 1482. *(page 311)*

12-29 Antonio del Pollaiuolo. *Battle of the Ten Nudes.* c. 1465–70. *(page 312)*

12-30 Martin Schongauer. *Temptation of Saint Anthony.* c. 1480–90. *(page 313)*

Chapter 13

Art of the High Renaissance and Reformation

Notes

Raphael. Stanza della Segnatura, Vatican, Rome. Right: *Philosophy* or *School of Athens* with Plato and Aristotle; left: (over the window) *Poetry and the Arts*, represented by Apollo and the Muses. 1510–11. *(page 314)*

BOX Leonardo da Vinci. *Vitruvian Man.* c. 1490. *(page 316)*

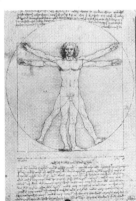

13-1 Leonardo da Vinci. *Last Supper,* wall painting in the Refectory, Monastery of Santa Maria delle Grazie, Milan. 1495–98. *(page 317)*

_____

_____

_____

_____

_____

_____

_____

_____

_____

_____

13-2 Leonardo da Vinci. *Mona Lisa.* c. 1503–06. *(page 318)*

_____

_____

_____

_____

_____

_____

_____

_____

_____

_____

_____

_____

13-3 Raphael. *The Small Cowper Madonna.* c. 1505. *(page 318)*

_____

_____

_____

_____

_____

_____

_____

_____

_____

_____

13-4 Raphael. *Disputà,* fresco in the Stanza della Segnatura, Vatican, Rome. 1510–11. *(page 319)*

13-5 Raphael. *School of Athens,* fresco in the Stanza della Segnatura, Vatican, Rome. 1510–11. *(page 320)*

13-6 Michelangelo. *Pietà,* from Old Saint Peter's. c. 1500. *(page 321)*

13-7 Michelangelo. *David.* 1501–04. *(page 322)*

_____

_____

_____

_____

_____

_____

_____

_____

_____

_____

13-8 Interior, Sistine Chapel, Vatican, Rome.
Built 1475–81. Ceiling painted 1508–12; wall
behind altar painted 1536–41. *(page 323)*

_____

_____

_____

_____

_____

_____

_____

_____

_____

_____

13-9 Michelangelo. Sistine Ceiling. Top to bottom: *Expulsion* (center); *Creation of Eve* with *Ezekiel* (left) and *Cumaean Sibyl* (right); *Creation of Adam* (middle); *God Gathering the Waters* with *Persian Sibyl* (left) and *Daniel* (right); and *God Creating the Sun, Moon, and Plants*. Frescoes on the ceiling, Sistine Chapel. 1508–12. *(page 324)*

_____

_____

_____

_____

_____

_____

_____

_____

_____

_____

13-10 Michelangelo. *Last Judgment,* Sistine Chapel, 1536–41. *(page 325)*

_____

_____

_____

_____

_____

_____

_____

_____

_____

13-11 Michelangelo. Saint Peter's Basilica, Vatican, Rome. c. 1546–64 (dome completed 1590 by Giacomo della Porta). View from the southwest. *(page 327)*

13-12 Michelangelo. *Pietà* (known as the *Rondanini Pietà*) 1555–64. *(page 328)*

13-13 Titian (formerly attributed to Giorgione). *Pastoral Concert* c. 1509–10. *(page 329)*

BOX Titian. *Isabella d'Este.* 1534–36. *(page 329)*

13-14 Titian. *Pesaro Madonna.* 1519–26.
(page 330)

13-15 Titian. *Venus of Urbino.* c. 1538.
(page 331)

13-16 Veronese. *Feast in the House of Levi,*
from the Monastery of Santi Giovanni e Paolo,
Venice. 1573. *(page 332)*

13-17 Tintoretto. *Last Supper.* 1592–94.
(page 333)

13-18 Palladio. Villa Rotonda (Villa Capra),
Vicenza, Italy. Begun 1550. *(page 334)*

13-19 Palladio Plan of the Villa Rotunda. *(page 334)*

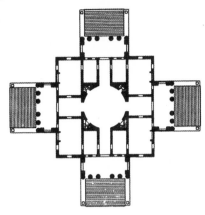

13-20 Capponi Chapel, Church of Santa Felicità, Florence Chapel by Filippo Brunelleschi, 1419–23; paintings by Pontormo, 1525–28. *(page 335)*

13-21 Pontormo. *Entombment.* 1525–28. *(page 335)*

13-22 Bronzino. *Portrait of a Young Man.*
c. 1540–45. *(page 336)*

13-23 Sofonisba Anguissola. *Child Bitten by a Crayfish.* c. 1558. *(page 337)*

13-24 Lavinia Fontana. *Noli Me Tangere.* c. 1581. *(page 337)*

13-25 Primaticcio. Stucco and wall painting, Chamber of the duchess of Étampes Château of Fontainebleau. 1540s. *(page 338)*

13-26 Benvenuto Cellini. *Saltcellar of Francis I of France* (container for salt and pepper). 1540–43. *(page 339)*

BOX Giacomo da Vignola and Giacomo della Porta. Facade elevation of the Church of Il Gesù, Rome. c. 1575–84. *(page 340)*

13-27 Giacomo da Vignola and Giacomo della Porta. Church of Il Gesù Facade, Rome. Begun on Vignola's design in 1568; completed by della Porta c. 1575–84. *(page 340)*

13-28 Matthias Grünewald. *Isenheim Altarpiece,* closed, from the Community of Saint Anthony, Isenheim, France. *Crucifixion* (center panel); *Lamentation* (predella); Saints Sebastian and Anthony Abbot (side panels). c. 1510–15. *(page 341)*

13-29 Albrecht Dürer. *Self-Portrait.* 1500. *(page 342)*

13-30 Albrecht Dürer. *Adam and Eve.* 1504. *(page 342)*

_____

_____

_____

_____

_____

_____

_____

_____

_____

_____

_____

13-31 Albrecht Dürer. *Four Apostles* 1526. *(page 343)*

_____

_____

_____

_____

_____

_____

_____

_____

_____

_____

13-32 Tilman Riemenschneider. *Altarpiece of the Holy Blood. Last Supper* (center); *Entry into Jerusalem* (left wing); *Agony in the Garden* (right wing); *The Annunciation* (upper figures), *The Resurrected Christ* (top-most figure). 1499–1505. *(page 344)*

_____

_____

_____

_____

_____

_____

_____

13-33 Hans Holbein the Younger. *Henry VIII.*
1540. *(page 345)*

_____
_____
_____
_____
_____
_____
_____
_____
_____
_____

13-34 Caterina van Hemessen. *Self-Portrait.*
1548. *(page 346)*

_____
_____
_____
_____
_____
_____
_____
_____
_____
_____
_____
_____

13-35 Hieronymus Bosch. *Garden of Earthly
Delights* (center); *Creation* (left wing); *The
Damned* (right wing). c. 1505–15. *(page 347)*

_____
_____
_____
_____
_____
_____
_____
_____
_____

13-36 Pieter Bruegel the Elder. *Hunters in the Snow.* 1565. *(page 348)*

13-37 El Greco. *Burial of Count Orgaz,* Church of Santo Tomé, Toledo, Spain. 1586. *(page 349)*

Chapter 14
Baroque and Rococo Art

Notes

Gianlorenzo Bernini. *Saint Teresa of Ávila in Ecstasy.* 1645–52. *(page 350)*

_____

_____

_____

_____

_____

_____

_____

_____

_____

_____

14-1 Gianlorenzo Bernini. *Baldacchino.* 1624–33. *(page 352)*

_____

_____

_____

_____

_____

_____

_____

_____

_____

_____

_____

_____

14-2 Gianlorenzo Bernini. Saint Peter's Basilica and Square. Vatican, Rome Carlo Maderno, facade 1607–15; Bernini, square designed c. 1656–57. *(page 353)*

14-3 Gianlorenzo Bernini. *David*. 1623. *(page 354)*

14-4 Gianlorenzo Bernini. Cornaro Chapel, Church of Santa Maria della Vittoria, Rome. 1642–52. *(page 354)*

14-5 Annibale Carracci. Ceiling fresco of main gallery, Palazzo Farnese, Rome. 1597–1601. *(page 355)*

14-6 Giovanni Battista Gaulli. *Triumph of the Name of Jesus,* ceiling fresco with stucco figures in the vault of the Church of Il Gesù, Rome. 1676–79. *(page 356)*

14-7 Caravaggio. *Calling of Saint Matthew* in the Contarelli Chapel, Church of San Luigi dei Francesi, Rome. 1599–1600. *(page 357)*

14-8 Artemisia Gentileschi. *La Pittura,* a self-portrait. 1630. *(page 358)*

14-9 Hyacinthe Rigaud. *Louis XIV.* 1701. *(page 359)*

14-10 Louis Le Vau and Jules Hardouin-Mansart. Palais de Versailles, Versailles, France. Gardens by André Le Nôtre. 1668–85. *(page 360)*

14-11 Jules Hardouin-Mansart and Charles Le Brun. Hall of Mirrors, Palais de Versailles. Begun 1678. *(page 361)*

14-12 Nicolas Poussin. *Landscape with Saint John on Patmos. 1640.* (page 362)

14-13 Diego Velázquez. *Water Carrier of Seville.* c. 1619. *(page 363)*

14-14 Diego Velázquez. *Las Meninas* (*The Maids of Honor*). 1656. *(page 364)*

BOX Pedro de Ribera. Facade elevation of the Portal of the Hospicio de San Fernando, Madrid. 1722. *(page 365)*

14-15 Pedro de Ribera. Portal of the Hospicio de San Fernando, Madrid. 1722. *(page 365)*

14-16 Peter Paul Rubens. *The Raising of the Cross*, painted for the Church of Saint Walpurga, Antwerp, Belgium. 1609–10. *(page 366)*

14-17 Peter Paul Rubens. *Henri IV Receiving the Portrait of Marie de' Medici.* 1621–25. *(page 367)*

14-18 Jan Brueghel and Peter Paul Rubens. *Sight*, from *Allegories of the Five Senses.* c. 1617–18. *(page 368)*

14-19 Anthony van Dyck. *Charles I at the Hunt* 1635. *(page 369)*

14-20 Interior, Banqueting House, Whitehall Palace. Ceiling painting of the apotheosis of King James and the glorification of the Stuart monarchy by Peter Paul Rubens. 1630–35. *(page 370)*

14-21 Rembrandt van Rijn. *Captain Frans Banning Cocq Mustering His Company* (*The Night Watch*). 1642. *(page 371)*

14-22 Rembrandt van Rijn. *The Three Crosses*
(first state) 1663. *(page 372)*

_____

_____

_____

_____

_____

_____

_____

_____

_____

_____

14-23 Rembrandt van Rijn. *Self-Portrait* 1659.
(page 372)

_____

_____

_____

_____

_____

_____

_____

_____

_____

_____

14-24 Judith Leyster. *Self-Portrait.* 1635.
(page 373)

_____

_____

_____

_____

_____

_____

_____

_____

_____

_____

14-25 Jan Vermeer. *Woman Holding a Balance.*
c. 1664. *(page 374)*

14-26 Emanuel de Witte. *Portuguese
Synagogue Amsterdam.* 1680. *(page 375)*

14-27 Meindert Hobbema. *Avenue at Middelharnis.*
1689. *(page 376)*

14-28 Rachel Ruysch. *Flower Still Life.* After 1700. *(page 377)*

14-29 Germain Boffrand. Salon de la Princesse, Hôtel de Soubise Paris. Begun 1732. *(page 378)*

14-30 Johann Balthasar Neumann. Kaisersaal (Imperial Hall), Residenz, Würzburg, Bavaria, Germany. 1719–44 Fresco decoration by Giovanni Battista Tiepolo. 1751–52. *(page 379)*

14-31 Jean-Antoine Watteau. *The Pilgrimage to Cythera.* 1717. *(page 380)*

14-32 Jean-Honoré Fragonard. *The Meeting,* from *The Progress of Love.* 1771–73. *(page 381)*

14-33 Anna Maria Sibylla Merian. *Plate 9* from *Dissertation in Insect Generations and Metamorphosis in Surinam.* 1719 (printed posthumously). *(page 381)*

Chapter 15
Art of the Americas

Notes

Tunic, from Peru. Inca, c. 1500 CE. *(page 384)*

_____

_____

_____

_____

_____

_____

_____

_____

_____

_____

15-1 Ceremonial center of the city of Teotihuacan, Mexico. Teotihuacan culture, c. 500 CE. *(page 386)*

_____

_____

_____

_____

_____

_____

_____

_____

_____

_____

_____

15-2 Plan of the ceremonial center of Teotihuacan. *(page 386)*

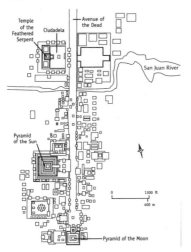

15-3 Temple of the Feathered Serpent, the Ciudadela, Teotihuacan Mexico. Teotihuacan culture, c. 350 CE. *(page 387)*

15-4 Palace (foreground) and Temple of the Inscriptions (tomb-pyramid of Lord Pacal), Palenque Mexico. Maya culture late 7th century CE. *(page 388)*

15-5 Portrait of Lord Pacal, from his tomb. Temple of the Inscriptions. Late 7th century CE. *(page 389)*

_____

_____

_____

_____

_____

_____

_____

_____

_____

_____

_____

15-6 Castillo, with Chacmool in foreground, Chichén Itzá, Yucatan, Mexico. Maya culture, 9th–13th century CE. *(page 389)*

_____

_____

_____

_____

_____

_____

_____

_____

_____

_____

15-7 *The Founding of Tenochtitlan,* page from *Codex Mendoza.* Aztec, 1540s CE. *(page 390)*

_____

_____

_____

_____

_____

_____

_____

_____

_____

_____

15-8 *The Moon Goddess, Coyolxauhqui.* Aztec, late 15th century CE. *(page 390)*

15-9 *The Mother Goddess, Coatlicue.* Aztec, late 15th century CE. *(page 391)*

15-10 Earth drawing of a hummingbird, Nazca Plain, southwest Peru. Nazca culture c. 100 BCE–700 CE. *(page 391)*

15-11 Machu Picchu Peru. Inca 15th–16th century CE. *(page 392)*

15-12 Tunic, from Peru. Inca, c. 1500 CE. *(page 393)*

15-13 Llama, from Bolivia or Peru, found near Lake Titicaca, Bolivia. Inca, 15th century CE. *(page 393)*

15-14 Sebastían Salcedo.*Our Lady of Guadalupe.* 1779. *(page 394)*

15-15 Beaver effigy platform pipe, from Bedford Mound Pike County, Illinois. Hopewell culture, c. 100–200 CE. *(page 395)*

15-16 Great Serpent Mound, Adams County, Ohio. c. 1070 CE. *(page 395)*

15-17 Reconstruction of central Cahokia. East St. Louis, Illinois. Mississippian culture, c. 1150 CE. *(page 395)*

_____

_____

_____

_____

_____

_____

_____

_____

_____

_____

15-18 Pueblo Bonito, Chaco Canyon, New Mexico. Anasazi culture, c. 900–1200 CE. *(page 396)*

_____

_____

_____

_____

_____

_____

_____

_____

_____

15-19 Seed jar. Anasazi culture, c. 1150 CE. *(page 396)*

_____

_____

_____

_____

_____

_____

_____

_____

_____

15-20 Maria Montoya Martínez and Julian Martínez.
Blackware storage jar, from San Ildefonso Pueblo,
New Mexico. Hopi c. 1942. *(page 396)*

15-21 Taos Pueblo, Tewa, Taos, New Mexico
Photographed by Laura Gilpin in 1947. *(page 397)*

BOX Feathered Bowl Wedding Basket. c. 1877.
(page 397)

15-22 Baby carrier, from the Upper Missouri River area. Eastern Sioux, 19th century. *(page 398)*

15-23 Blackfoot women raising a tepee. Photographed c. 1900. *(page 398)*

15-24 Hamatsa dancers, Kwakwaka'wakw (Kwakiutl) Canada. Photographed 1914 by Edward S. Curtis. *(page 399)*

15-25 Kwakwaka'wakw (Kwakiutl) Bird mask, from Alert Bay, Canada. Prior to 1951. *(page 400)*

15-26 Chilkat blanket. Tlingit, before 1928. *(page 400)*

15-27 Bill Reid. *The Spirit of Haida Gwaii.* Haida,1991. *(page 401)*

Chapter 16
African Art

Notes

Kojo Bonsu (attributed). Finial of a spokesperson's staff (*okyeame poma*), from an Akan kingdom, Ghana Asante culture, 20th century. *(page 402)*

_____

_____

_____

_____

_____

_____

_____

_____

_____

_____

16-1 Head. Nok style, from Nigeria. c. 500 BCE–200 CE. *(page 404)*

_____

_____

_____

_____

_____

_____

_____

_____

_____

_____

_____

16-2 Head of a king (oni), from Ife, Nigeria. Yoruba culture c. 12th–15th century. *(page 404)*

16-3 Head of an *oba* (king), from Benin, Nigeria. Edo culture c. 1700–1897 CE (Late Period). *(page 405)*

16-4 *General and Officers*, from Benin, Nigeria. 17th century. *(page 406)*

16-5 Pendant representing an *iyoba*, from Benin,
Nigeria. Edo culture, c. 1550 CE. *(page 406)*

16-6 Conical Tower, Great Zimbabwe. Before
1450 CE. *(page 407)*

16-7 Bird, top part of a monolith, from Great
Zimbabwe c. 1200–1400 CE. *(page 408)*

16-8 Jar, from Mali. Bamana culture, 20th century. *(page 410)*

16-9 Power figure (*nkisi nkonde*), from the Democratic Republic of the Congo (formerly Zaire). Kongo culture 19th century. *(page 410)*

16-10 Spirit spouse (*blolo bla*), from Ivory Coast. Baule culture Early 20th century. *(page 410)*

16-11 Olówè of Isè. Door from Yoruba royal palace in Ikéré Nigeria. c. 1925. *(page 411)*

16-12 *Kente* cloth, from Ghana. Asante culture, 20th century. *(page 412)*

16-13 Two masks in performance, from Dossi Burkina Faso. Bwa culture, 1984. *(page 413)*

16-14 Twin figures (*ere ibeji*), from Nigeria.
Yoruba culture, 20th century. *(page 413)*

_____

_____

_____

_____

_____

_____

_____

_____

_____

_____

_____

Chapter 17
Neoclassicism, Romanticism, and Realism

Notes

John Henry Fuseli. *The Nightmare.* 1781.
(page 416)

_____

_____

_____

_____

_____

_____

_____

_____

_____

_____

17-1 Antonio Canova. *Cupid and Psyche.*
1787–93. *(page 418)*

_____

_____

_____

_____

_____

_____

_____

_____

_____

_____

17-2 Marie-Louise-Élisabeth Vigée-Lebrun. *Portrait of Marie Antoinette with Her Children.* 1787. *(page 419)*

17-3 Adélaïde Labille-Guiard. *Self-Portrait with Two Pupils, Mademoiselle Marie Gabrielle Capet (1761–1818) and Mademoiselle Carreaux de Rosemond (d. 1788).* 1785. *(page 420)*

17-4 Thomas Gainsborough. *Portrait of Mrs. Richard Brinsley Sheridan.* 1785–87. *(page 421)*

BOX Johann Zoffany. *Academicians of the Royal Academy.* 1771–72. *(page 422)*

_____

_____

_____

_____

_____

_____

_____

_____

_____

_____

17-5 John Singleton Copley. *Mrs. Ezekiel Goldthwait (Elizabeth Lewis).* 1771. *(page 423)*

_____

_____

_____

_____

_____

_____

_____

_____

_____

_____

_____

_____

17-6 William Hogarth. *The Marriage Contract* from *Marriage à la Mode.* 1743–45. *(page 423)*

_____

_____

_____

_____

_____

_____

_____

_____

_____

_____

_____

17-7 Angelica Kauffmann. *Cornelia Pointing to Her Children as Her Treasures.* 1785. *(page 424)*

17-8 Joseph Wright. *An Experiment on a Bird in the Air-Pump.* 1768. *(page 425)*

17-9 Robert Adam. Anteroom, Syon House, Middlesex England. 1760–69. *(page 426)*

17-10 Thomas Jefferson. Monticello, near
Charlottesville, Virginia. 1770–84, 1796–1806.
(page 426)

17-11 Jacques-Louis David. *Oath of the Horatii.*
1784–85. *(page 427)*

17-12 Jacques-Louis David. *Napoleon Crossing
the Saint-Bernard.* 1800–01. *(page 427)*

17-13 Jean-Auguste-Dominique Ingres. *Large Odalisque.* 1814. *(page 428)*

_____

_____

_____

_____

_____

_____

_____

_____

_____

_____

17-14 Jean-Auguste-Dominique Ingres. *The Comtesse d'Haussonville.* Dated 1845. *(page 428)*

_____

_____

_____

_____

_____

_____

_____

_____

_____

_____

17-15 Théodore Géricault. *Raft of the "Medusa."* 1818–19. *(page 429)*

_____

_____

_____

_____

_____

_____

_____

_____

17-16 Eugène Delacroix. *Women of Algiers*
1834. *(page 430)*

17-17 Francisco Goya. *The Sleep of Reason
Produces Monsters*, No. 43 from *Los Caprichos
(The Caprices)* 1796–98. *(page 430)*

17-18 Francisco Goya *Family of Charles IV.*
1800. *(page 431)*

17-19 Francisco Goya. *Third of May, 1808.*
1814–15. *(page 432)*

17-20 John Henry Fuseli. *The Nightmare.* 1781.
(page 432)

17-21 John Constable. *The White Horse* 1819.
(page 433)

BOX William Hackwood, for Josiah Wedgwood.
"Am I Not a Man and a Brother?" 1787. *(page 433)*

_____

_____

_____

_____

_____

_____

_____

_____

_____

_____

17-22 Joseph Mallord William Turner. *The Fighting "Téméraire," Tugged to Her Last Berth to Be Broken Up.* 1838. *(page 434)*

_____

_____

_____

_____

_____

_____

_____

_____

_____

_____

17-23 Louis-Jacques-Mandé Daguerre. *The Artist's Studio* 1837. *(page 435)*

_____

_____

_____

_____

_____

_____

_____

_____

_____

_____

17-24 William Henry Fox Talbot. *The Open Door.* 1843. *(page 435)*

_____

_____

_____

_____

_____

_____

_____

_____

_____

_____

_____

17-25 Julia Margaret Cameron. *Portrait of Thomas Carlyle.* 1863. *(page 435)*

_____

_____

_____

_____

_____

_____

_____

_____

_____

_____

_____

17-26 Rosa Bonheur. *Plowing in the Nivernais: The Dressing of the Vines.* 1849. *(page 437)*

_____

_____

_____

_____

_____

_____

_____

_____

_____

_____

17-27 Gustave Courbet. *A Burial at Ornans.*
1849. *(page 437)*

17-28 Ilya Repin. *Bargehaulers on the Volga.*
1870–73. *(page 438)*

17-29 John James Audubon. *Common Grackle,* for
The Birds of America. 1826–39. *(page 439)*

17-30 George Caleb Bingham. *Fur Traders Descending the Missouri.* c. 1845. *(page 439)*

_____

_____

_____

_____

_____

_____

_____

_____

_____

_____

_____

Chapter 18
Later Nineteenth-Century Art in Europe and the United States

Notes

Georges Serat. *A Sunday Afternoon on the Island of La Grande Jatte.* 1884–86. *(page 441)*

_____

_____

_____

_____

_____

_____

_____

_____

_____

_____

18-1 Abraham Darby III. The Severn River Bridge, Coalbrookdale, England. Completed 1779. *(page 442)*

_____

_____

_____

_____

_____

_____

_____

_____

_____

18-2 Louis Sullivan. Wainwright Building St.
Louis, Missouri. 1890–91. *(page 443)*

_____

_____

_____

_____

_____

_____

_____

_____

_____

18-3 Gustave Eiffel. Eiffel Tower, Paris. 1887–89.
(page 443)

_____

_____

_____

_____

_____

_____

_____

_____

_____

_____

18-4 Harriet Hosmer. Zenobia in Chains. 1859.
(page 444)

_____

_____

_____

_____

_____

_____

_____

_____

_____

18-5 Edmonia Lewis. *Hagar in the Wilderness.*
1875. *(page 445)*

_____

_____

_____

_____

_____

_____

_____

_____

_____

_____

18-6 Dante Gabriel Rossetti. *La Pia de' Tolomei.*
1868–69. *(page 446)*

_____

_____

_____

_____

_____

_____

_____

_____

_____

_____

18-7 *(foreground in photo)* Philip Webb (?). Single
chair from the Sussex range. In production from
c. 1865. *(background)* William Morris. Peacock and
Dragon curtain 1878. *(page 447)*

_____

_____

_____

_____

_____

_____

_____

_____

_____

_____

18-8 Victor Horta. Stairway, *Tassel House,*
Brussels. 1892–93. *(page 448)*

_____

_____

_____

_____

_____

_____

_____

_____

_____

_____

18-9 Antoni Gaudí. Serpentine bench, Güell
Park, Barcelona. 1900–14. *(page 448)*

_____

_____

_____

_____

_____

_____

_____

_____

_____

_____

18-10 Timothy H. O'Sullivan. *Ancient Ruins in
the Cañon de Chelley, Arizona.* 1873. *(page 449)*

_____

_____

_____

_____

_____

_____

_____

_____

_____

18-11 Winslow Homer. Snap the Whip. 1872.
(page 450)

_____

_____

_____

_____

_____

_____

_____

_____

_____

_____

_____

18-12 Thomas Eakins. *The Gross Clinic.* 1875.
(page 450)

_____

_____

_____

_____

_____

_____

_____

_____

_____

_____

_____

_____

_____

18-13 Albert Pinkham Ryder. *Jonah.* c. 1885.
(page 450)

_____

_____

_____

_____

_____

_____

_____

_____

_____

_____

18-14 Édouard Manet. *Le Déjeuner sur l'herbe (The Luncheon on the Grass).* 1863. *(page 451)*

18-15 Édouard Manet. *Olympia.* 1863. *(page 452)*

18-16 Claude Monet. *Boulevard des Capucines, Paris* 1873–74. *(page 453)*

18-17 Berthe Morisot. *In the Dining Room.*
1886. *(page 454)*

_____

_____

_____

_____

_____

_____

_____

_____

_____

_____

18-18 Edgar Degas. *The Rehearsal of the
Ballet on Stage.* c. 1874. *(page 454)*

_____

_____

_____

_____

_____

_____

_____

_____

_____

_____

18-19 Édouard Manet. *A Bar at the Folies-
Bergère.* 1881–82. *(page 455)*

_____

_____

_____

_____

_____

_____

_____

_____

_____

18-20 Pierre-Auguste Renoir. *Luncheon of the Boating Party.* 1881. *(page 456)*

18-21 Mary Cassatt. *Maternal Caress* 1891. *(page 456)*

18-22 Claude Monet. *Water Lilies.* c. 1920. *(page 457)*

18-23 Paul Cézanne. *Mont Sainte-Victoire.*
c. 1885–87. *(page 458)*

18-24 Paul Cézanne. *Still Life with Basket of Apples.* 1890–94. *(page 458)*

18-25 Georges Seurat. Detail of *A Sunday Afternoon on the Island of La Grande Jatte.* *(page 459)*

18-26 Paul Gauguin. *Ia Orana Maria (We Hail Thee Mary).* c. 1891–92. *(page 460)*

_____

_____

_____

_____

_____

_____

_____

_____

_____

_____

18-27 Vincent van Gogh. *Sunflowers.* 1888. *(page 461)*

_____

_____

_____

_____

_____

_____

_____

_____

_____

_____

18-28 Vincent van Gogh. *The Starry Night.* 1889. *(Page 461)*

_____

_____

_____

_____

_____

_____

_____

_____

_____

_____

18-29 Henri de Toulouse-Lautrec. *Jane Avril.*
1893. *(page 462)*

_____

_____

_____

_____

_____

_____

_____

_____

_____

_____

18-30 Paul Signac. *Plane Trees, Place des
Lices, Saint-Tropez, Opus 242.* 1893. *(page 463)*

_____

_____

_____

_____

_____

_____

_____

_____

_____

_____

_____

18-31 Auguste Rodin. *Burghers of Calais.*
1884–86. *(page 464)*

_____

_____

_____

_____

_____

_____

_____

_____

_____

_____

18-32 Camille Claudel. *The Waltz.* 1892–1905.
(page 465)

Chapter 19
Modern Art:
Europe and North America
in the Early Twentieth Century

Notes

Marcel Duchamp. *The Bride Stripped Bare by Her Bachelors, Even (The Large Glass).* 1915–23. *(page 466)*

_____

_____

_____

_____

_____

_____

_____

_____

_____

_____

19-1 Edvard Munch. *The Scream.* 1893. *(page 468)*

_____

_____

_____

_____

_____

_____

_____

_____

_____

19-2 Paula Modersohn-Becker. *Self-Portrait with an Amber Necklace.* 1906. *(page 469)*

BOX Pierre Legrain. Tabouret. c. 1923. *(page 470)*

BOX Chair, Ngombe artist, Democratic Republic of the Congo. *(page 470)*

19-3 Käthe Schmidt Kollwitz. *The Outbreak,* from the
Peasants' War series. 1903. *(page 470)*

19-4 Henri Matisse. *The Joy of Life.* 1905–06.
(page 471)

19-5 Ernst Ludwig Kirchner. *Street, Berlin.* 1913.
(page 472)

19-6 Vasily Kandinsky. *Improvisation No. 30 (Cannons).* 1913. *(page 473)*

19-7 Paul Klee. *Hammamet with Its Mosque.* 1914. *(page 474)*

19-8 Pablo Picasso. *Les Demoiselles d'Avignon.* 1907. *(page 475)*

19-9 Georges Braque. *Violin and Palette.*
1909–10. *(page 476)*

_____

_____

_____

_____

_____

_____

_____

_____

_____

_____

_____

19-10 Pablo Picasso. *Ma Jolie.* 1911–12.
(page 476)

_____

_____

_____

_____

_____

_____

_____

_____

_____

_____

_____

19-11 Pablo Picasso. *Glass and Bottle of Suze.*
1912. *(page 477)*

_____

_____

_____

_____

_____

_____

_____

_____

_____

_____

_____

19-12 Sonia Delaunay-Terk. Clothes and customized Citroën B-12. From *Maison de la Mode*, 1925. *(page 478)*

19-13 Umberto Boccioni. *Unique Forms of Continuity in Space.* 1913. *(page 478)*

19-14 Natalia Goncharova. *Aeroplane over Train.* 1913. *(page 479)*

19-15 Kazimir Malevich. *Suprematist Painting
(Eight Red Rectangles).* 1915. *(page 479)*

19-16 Alfred Stieglitz. *Spring Showers.* 1901.
(page 480)

19-17 Max Weber. *Rush Hour, New York.* 1915.
(page 480)

19-18 Henry Moore. *Recumbent Figure.* 1938.
(page 481)

19-19 El Lissitzky. Proun space created for a
Berlin art exhibition. 1923, reconstruction 1965.
(page 482)

19-20 Piet Mondrian. *Composition with Red,
Blue, and Yellow.* 1930. *(page 483)*

19-21 Gerrit Rietveld. Interior, Schröder House,
Utrecht, the Netherlands. 1924. *(page 483)*

19-22 Charles-Édouard Jeanneret (Le Corbusier). Plan
for a Contemporary City of Three Million Inhabitants.
1922 (From *Oeuvre complete*, 1910–29). *(page 484)*

19-23 Walter Gropius. Bauhaus Building,
Dessau, Germany. 1925–26. *(page 484)*

19-24 Ludwig Mies van der Rohe. Interior, German pavilion International Exposition, Barcelona, 1929. *(page 485)*

19-25 Frank Lloyd Wright. Edgar Kaufmann House, Fallingwater. Mill Run, Pennsylvania 1935–37. *(page 486)*

19-26 Hugo Ball reciting the sound poem "Karawane." Photographed at the Cabaret Voltaire, Zürich, 1916. *(page 486)*

BOX Room 3 of "Degenerate Art" exhibition,
Munich, 1937. *(page 487)*

_____

_____

_____

_____

_____

_____

_____

_____

_____

_____

_____

19-27 Marcel Duchamp. *Fountain.* 1917. *(page 488)*

_____

_____

_____

_____

_____

_____

_____

_____

_____

_____

_____

_____

_____

19-28 Marcel Duchamp. *The Bride Stripped
Bare by Her Bachelors, Even (The Large
Glass).* 1915–23. *(page 488)*

_____

_____

_____

_____

_____

_____

_____

_____

_____

_____

_____

19-29 Pablo Picasso. *Guernica.* 1937. *(page 489)*

19-30 Salvador Dalí. *The Persistence of Memory.*
1931. *(page 490)*

19-31 Joan Miró. *Dutch Interior I.* 1928.
(page 491)

19-32 Alexander Calder. *Lobster Trap and Fish Tail.* 1939. *(page 491)*

_____

_____

_____

_____

_____

_____

_____

_____

_____

_____

_____

19-33 Charles Sheeler. *American Landscape.* 1930. *(page 492)*

_____

_____

_____

_____

_____

_____

_____

_____

_____

_____

_____

19-34 Grant Wood. *American Gothic.* 1930. *(page 493)*

_____

_____

_____

_____

_____

_____

_____

_____

_____

_____

_____

19-35 Dorothea Lange. *Migrant Mother, Nipomo California.* February 1936. *(page 494)*

19-36 Aaron Douglas. *Aspects of Negro Life: From Slavery Through Reconstruction.* 1934. *(page 494)*

19-37 James VanDerZee. Detail of *Couple Wearing Raccoon Coats with a Cadillac, Taken on West 127th Street, Harlem, New York.* 1932. *(page 495)*

19-38 Diego Rivera. *Man, Controller of the Universe.* 1934. *(page 496)*

19-39 Frida Kahlo *The Two Fridas* 1939. *(page 496).*

19-40 Emily Carr. *Big Raven.* 1931. *(page 497)*

Chapter 20
Art Since 1945

Notes

Maya Ying Lin. *Vietnam Veterans Memorial.*
1982. *(page 498)*

_____

_____

_____

_____

_____

_____

_____

_____

_____

_____

_____

20-1 Antoni Tàpies. *White with Graphism.*
1957. *(page 500)*

_____

_____

_____

_____

_____

_____

_____

_____

_____

_____

_____

20-2 Arshile Gorky. *Garden in Sochi.* c. 1943. *(page 501)*

20-3 Jackson Pollock. *Autumn Rhythm (Number 30).* 1950. *(page 502)*

20-4 Lee Krasner. *The Seasons.* 1957. *(page 502)*

20-5 Willem de Kooning. *Woman I.* 1950–52. *(page 503)*

_____

_____

_____

_____

_____

_____

_____

_____

_____

_____

_____

_____

20-6 Mark Rothko. *Brown, Blue, Brown on Blue.* 1953. *(page 504)*

_____

_____

_____

_____

_____

_____

_____

_____

_____

_____

_____

20-7 Helen Frankenthaler. *Mountains and Sea.* 1952. *(page 504)*

_____

_____

_____

_____

_____

_____

_____

_____

_____

20-8 Louise Nevelson. *Sky Cathedral.* 1958.
(page 505)

_____

_____

_____

_____

_____

_____

_____

_____

_____

_____

_____

20-9 Robert Rauschenburg. *Canyon.* 1959.
(page 506)

_____

_____

_____

_____

_____

_____

_____

_____

_____

_____

_____

_____

20-10 Jasper Johns. *Target with Four Faces.*
1955 *(page 507)*

_____

_____

_____

_____

_____

_____

_____

_____

_____

_____

20-11 Jean Tinguely. *Homage to New York.* 1960. *(page 508)*

_____

_____

_____

_____

_____

_____

_____

_____

_____

_____

_____

20-12 Roy Lichtenstein. *Oh, Jeff . . . I Love You, Too . . . But . . .* 1964. *(page 508)*

_____

_____

_____

_____

_____

_____

_____

_____

_____

_____

_____

_____

_____

20-13 Andy Warhol. *Marilyn Diptych.* 1962. *(page 509)*

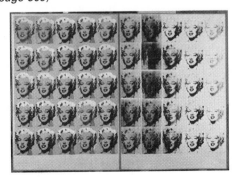

_____

_____

_____

_____

_____

_____

_____

20-14 Claes Oldenburg. *Lipstick (Ascending) on Caterpillar Tracks.* 1969, reworked 1974. *(page 509)*

20-15 Bridget Riley. *Current.* 1964. *(page 510)*

20-16 Donald Judd. *Untitled.* 1969. *(page 510)*

20-17 Eva Hesse. *Rope Piece* 1969–70.
(page 511)

20-18 Joseph Kosuth. *One and Three Chairs.*
1965. *(page 511)*

20-19 Bruce Nauman. *Self-Portrait as a
Fountain.* 1966–67. *(page 512)*

20-20 Peter Voulkos. *Untitled Plate.* 1962.
(page 512)

_____

_____

_____

_____

_____

_____

_____

_____

_____

_____

20-21 Ludwig Mies van der Rohe and Philip Johnson.
Seagram Building, New York City. 1954–58. *(page 513)*

_____

_____

_____

_____

_____

_____

_____

_____

_____

_____

_____

20-22 Robert Venturi and Denise Scott Brown.
Stair Hall with Ming dynasty tomb figures, The
Seattle Art Museum. 1986–91. *(page 514)*

_____

_____

_____

_____

_____

_____

_____

_____

_____

_____

20-23 Norman Foster. Hongkong & Shanghai Bank, Hong Kong. 1979–86. *(page 514)*

20-24 Frank O. Gehry. Guggenheim Museum, Bilbao, Spain. 1993–97. *(page 514)*

20-25 Robert Smithson. *Spiral Jetty.* 1969–70. *(page 515)*

20-26 Miriam Schapiro. *Personal Appearance #3*. 1973. *(page 516)*

20-27 Judy Chicago. *The Dinner Party*. 1974–79. *(page 516)*

20-28 Betye Saar. *The Liberation of Aunt Jemima*. 1972. *(page 517)*

20-29 Cindy Sherman. *Untitled Film Still.* 1978.
(page 518)

20-30 Elizabeth Murray. *Chaotic Lip.* 1986.
(page 518)

20-31 Anselm Kiefer. *Märkischer Heide.* 1984.
(page 519)

20-32 Magdalena Abakanowicz. *Backs.* 1976–80. *(page 519)*

20-33 Kiki Smith. *Untitled.* 1988. *(page 519)*

20-34 Martin Puryear. *Plenty's Boast.* 1994–95. *(page 520)*

20-35 Wendell Castle. *Ghost Clock.* 1985.
(page 520)

_____

_____

_____

_____

_____

_____

_____

_____

_____

_____

20-36 Clifford Possum Tjapaltjarri. *Man's Love Story.* 1978. *(page 521)*

_____

_____

_____

_____

_____

_____

_____

_____

_____

_____

_____

20-37 Jaune Quick-to-See Smith. *Trade (Gifts for Trading Land with White People).* Salish-Cree-Shoshone, 1992. *(page 522)*

_____

_____

_____

_____

_____

_____

_____

_____

_____

20-38 Jenny Holzer. *Untitled (Selections from Truisms, Inflammatory Essays, The Living Series, The Survival Series, Under a Rock, Laments, and Mother and Child Text).* 1989–90. *(page 523)*

20-39 Nam June Paik. *Electronic Superhighway: Continental U.S.* 1995. *(page 524)*

20-40 Bill Viola. *The Crossing.* 1996. *(page 524)*

20-41 Shirin Neshat Production still from *Fervor*. 2000. *(page 525)*

20-42 Maya Ying Lin. *Vietnam Veterans Memorial*. 1982. *(page 525)*

20-43 Digital rendering of the *Tribute in Light* memorial by artists Julian LaVerdiere and Paul Myoda as it appears on the cover of *Art in America*, November 2001. *(page 526)*